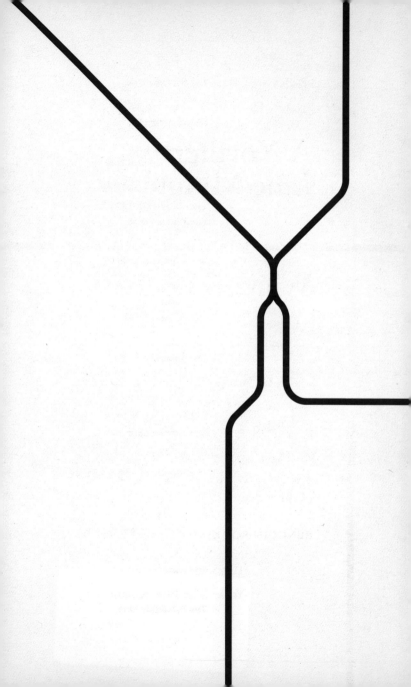

A Northern
Line Minute

William Leith

PENGUIN BOOKS

PENGUIN BOOKS

Published by the Penguin Group
Penguin Books Ltd, 80 Strand, London WC2R ORL, England
Penguin Group (USA) Inc., 375 Hudson Street, New York, New York 10014, USA
Penguin Group (Canada), 90 Eglinton Avenue East, Suite 700, Toronto, Ontario,
Canada M4P 2Y3 (a division of Pearson Penguin Canada Inc.)
Penguin Ireland, 25 St Stephen's Green, Dublin 2, Ireland (a division of Penguin Books Ltd)
Penguin Group (Australia), 707 Collins Street, Melbourne, Victoria 3008, Australia
(a division of Pearson Australia Group Pty Ltd)
Penguin Books India Pvt Ltd, 11 Community Centre, Panchsheel Park, New Delhi – 110 017, India
Penguin Group (NZ), 67 Apollo Drive, Rosedale, Auckland 0632, New Zealand
(a division of Pearson New Zealand Ltd)
Penguin Books (South Africa) (Pty) Ltd, Block D, Rosebank Office Park, 181 Jan Smuts Avenue,
Parktown North, Gauteng 2193, South Africa

Penguin Books Ltd, Registered Offices: 80 Strand, London WC2R ORL, England

www.penguin.com

First published in Penguin Books 2013
001

Set in 11.75/15pt Baskerville MT Std
Typeset by Jouve (UK), Milton Keynes
Printed in England by Clays Ltd, St Ives plc

ISBN: 978-1-846-14531-5

www.greenpenguin.co.uk

Penguin Books is committed to a sustainable
future for our business, our readers and our planet.
This book is made from Forest Stewardship
Council™ certified paper.

ALWAYS LEARNING   **PEARSON**

I'm on the train, and the doors are shutting behind me, when I smell the smoke; or rather I'm stepping into the train, towards the seating area, when I sense something bad, and I don't know what it is, and I sit down, and I see that the doors are shutting, and I don't know yet where the bad feeling is coming from, because when you smell something it goes straight to your memory, smell bypasses all analysis, as Proust described when he bit into the dunked cake and was transported to his childhood, and only later realized that this was because of the smell of the cake, the madeleine; I step into the train, and feel the bad feeling, the ominous feeling, that something is very wrong, it's the memory of fires, but not good fires, and I sit down in the seat, and the doors close, and then I realize that I'm smelling something, and it's burning rubber, or plastic, or oil, or a mixture of all three, and I shift upwards in my seat, already knowing it's too late, because the doors are closing; have closed.

Here I am on a Northern Line train at Belsize Park Station, and I'm carrying a plastic bag, and wearing a jacket but no coat, because it's a warm day in the spring, in the 1990s, and my first thought, after I think I can smell burning rubber, or plastic, is that I must be mistaken, I have to be mistaken, I'm anxious about the Underground, have in fact only just started to use it again after two years of not being able to, eighteen months of not going into the stations at all, and six months of buying tickets every so often, and getting on to the platform, and not being able to get on the train, the platform appearing to close around me as the train approached; I would watch the doors open, and then close, and then I'd watch the train move into the tunnel, a tight squeeze, and I'd move back towards the lift, lift 1 or lift 2, mostly at Belsize Park, and feel an icy tingle in my spine as I got into the lift, and the lift would rise, a very long minute, what people call a Northern Line minute, and I'd get back out of the lift, and wait for the doors to open, and I'd walk out into the tiny concourse, feeling shaky, and there would be an overwhelming sense of relief when I saw the sky for the first time after being down in that tunnel.

So the first thing I do, after feeling bad, and after thinking I've smelled the smoke, is to tell myself that I'm not smelling burning rubber, or plastic, or, alternatively, that I am smelling burning plastic or rubber, but that this is normal; down here, in these tunnels, smells like this are normal, in the same way that the smell of roasting meat is normal in a restaurant, or someone's kitchen; down here, in these tunnels, things are different, the puffs of strange-smelling wind, the warm and cold air, it's like an alien weather system, and, what's more, the smell of slightly singed engine materials, or engine-housing materials, is only to be expected; I tell myself I'm not used to being down here, it's been a struggle to get this far, and now I'm on the train, for the third or fourth time, I've conquered my fear, and this mild panic at the smell of normal things normally being singed in the course of hauling these carriages through these tunnels is fine, absolutely fine.

And now the train hisses, or sneezes, and very slightly lurches, and begins taxiing along the platform, getting up to full speed, and I try to relax into my seat, try to re-imagine that feeling of hope and mild excitement I normally relish as the craft I'm in starts up; I normally love it as an overground train pulls out of a station, and I look out of the window, and breathe out, and watch the backs of houses, the glinting windows, and I quite like it when planes take off, the feeling of tremendous anxiety muffled by the heavy load of denial one must use to deal with the vision of the ground angling away from you, and I sometimes feel a similar thing in the passenger seat in a car, fiddling with the window to give myself a sense of control. But I can't muster any of those feelings now; I know I must just look around me, and grit the journey out. People never tell you to have a pleasant journey on the Underground, just as people will say 'enjoy your meal', but never 'enjoy your cigarette' if you're a smoker, which I'm not.

I'm heading for Tottenham Court Road, in the West End of London, to see a film, and I'm late, and I might or might not have time to buy a coffee in a cardboard cup to take into the film; I might have to watch the film without caffeine, is what I'm thinking as the tiled, lighted platform, for so long a place of fear, gives way to a more novel view – the dark, cabled wall of the tunnel.

Breathing in again, and now definitely acknowledging, being unable not to acknowledge, the smell of burning rubber or plastic, my brain struggles to interpret this information

in a positive way. It smells so very wrong, the
sort of thing you might expect on amateur or
specialist transport, somebody's weekend boat,
or the car two boys made at school, using an
engine and bits of scaffolding as a chassis, you
could see them sometimes driving it around
the school, an engineering project that was a
spectacular success; you'd have expected *that*
sort of thing to produce an acrid stink, although
it didn't, and now I can remember the last time
I smelled something close to this exact smell,
in 1982, when, as a student, I borrowed my
mother's car, she was abroad, and I said I would
drive it back on the day she got back, and I had
200 miles to drive, which was fine at first, until
the car started smelling, because smoke was
coming out of the engine, but I decided to press
on, thinking that getting home on time was the
main thing; after a while the car slowed down,
and the smoke got blacker and denser, but still
I drove, crunching through the gears, the car
getting increasingly sluggish; with fifty miles
to go I felt that stopping would be a problem,

because I wouldn't be able to start it up again, so I forced the issue, feeling embarrassed in towns because of the smoke coming from the engine, and also the noise; the engine started grinding and chuntering, but I felt good as I entered the last few miles, believing that I would make it on time, that she'd arrive back from the airport, and I'd be there not long after, having triumphed over this minor adversity, and when I pulled into the drive, and walked into the house, I was surprised that the first thing she wanted to do was inspect the car – that's not what you do, I thought, when someone comes to visit, you don't say, hang on a minute, I know I haven't seen you for ages, but first let me inspect your car, but that's what she did, immediately becoming aware of the dense black smoke coming out of the front of the car, the smells of burning rubber and plastic, and oil and metal, which is almost exactly, but not quite, the smell that's in my nostrils now. The car smell was sweeter, sweatier. This is sharper and denser. This is worse.

But, as the train moves, at what feels like full speed, with slight turbulence, through the tunnel, I am still nowhere near full, or blind, panic – I am simply experiencing a rising sense of anxiety. I am, for instance, still in control of my thoughts. I clutch at my plastic bag, which contains a copy of a book, *American Psycho* by Bret Easton Ellis; I never go anywhere without a book, having a book to flip through is a great comfort, in virtually any situation; I'm reading this book for the third or fourth time, and can remember the first time I read it, on a plane from London to Miami, where I would see what I thought were the Bee Gees' houses, the three brothers having bought houses next to each other on the waterfront, and as I read this book for the first time, about a maniac financier who kills people, particularly women, and scoops out their brains, or more likely fantasizes about killing people and scooping out their brains, the person next to me, a woman from Miami, told me she knew the book must be good, because I was reading it with such intensity, and as she

said this she looked over at the book, entering
my personal space, and I snapped the book
shut, because I was on a scene in which the
narrator was talking about scooping someone's
brain out, and when I snapped the book shut,
the woman gave me an odd look, and I could
not work out whether this was because I'd
snapped the book shut, which was bad enough,
or because she'd read part of the text, and was
now wondering about this person sitting next
to her intensely being so abjectly focused on
such utter filth, such utter perversion, which is
what I thought that she, who was wearing pastel
colours and too much make-up, would have
thought; she might not have bought the idea that,
actually, it's an allegorical work, a devastating
critique of the way financiers think and behave.
I put the book away in the elasticated seat
pocket in front of me, among the flight magazines
and the sick bag, and felt my anxiety rise,
because now, suddenly ripped from the world
that had been occupying my mind, of people's
heads being scooped out by a maniac, I started

to notice the facts of my situation, of being in a steel tube, moving through slightly turbulent air.

I've always been a nervous flyer, although, unlike with the Underground, this never actually stopped me using planes. Is this because my fear of heights is less intense than my fear of depths? Possibly. But, if I'm ever asked what I'm frightened of, my first instinct is to say that I'm frightened of heights. I don't like glass lifts, or the Eiffel Tower, or cliff paths – walking along the Seven Sisters, in Sussex, a broad undulating path with fields on one side, and a sheer drop on the other, is a very uncomfortable experience for me; even when I'm yards from the edge, I can think of nothing else, as if I'm being drawn towards it – the distance between me and the edge seems to be permanently shrinking, even when I'm measuring it with my eye, and can tell, rationally, that it is not. Something about being near the edge makes me wonder how close to the edge I could get without actually falling off, and this, in turn, makes me feel sick and dizzy. So I try to pretend to myself that the edge is not there at all; that, in fact, there are fields on both sides of the path, which is similar to what I do when I'm on a plane. I simply pretend I'm not on a plane. I immerse myself in a book, or a movie, or else, if I'm tired, I drink.

But drinking on the Underground would be quite wrong – drinking on the Underground is a complete no-no. If you see somebody drinking on an Underground train, you automatically despise them – unless they are Johnny Depp or something. Which is funny – on planes, the staff will serve you enough booze to get you pretty drunk. More Champagne, Sir? Mostly it's okay. You arrive, dazed and confused – but then, you'd be pretty dazed and confused anyway, after ten or twelve hours in the pressurized cabin, landing in a new time zone, with new weather and the smells of cleaning fluids, always the first thing you smell when you enter a new country – Clorox, I think, being the smell of America, or possibly Clorox B.

In the tunnel, clutching my bag, but not taking out my book, kneading and wrinkling

the plastic between my fingers, I again smell
the burning rubber or plastic smell, and even
though it's stronger, I'm still fighting against
my better instinct, which tells me I'm in danger,
possibly desperate danger, that this, in fact, is
what I was frightened of all along, a fire in an
Underground tunnel – King's Cross! – with
smoke and shouting and confusion and being
burned to death. I have no idea whatsoever
what it would feel like, being burned to death,
which is why, when you see somebody in a
movie being burned at the stake, you begin
to lose empathy for the victim the moment
they are engulfed in flames. It's almost a relief.
There's Joan of Arc, being dragged towards
the pyre, being strapped down, and the pyre
is lit – these moments are horrible. But then –
woof! – the flames engulf her. Phew! It's over!
Which is something you don't think, say, during
Marathon Man, when Laurence Olivier, as the
Nazi dentist, drills into Dustin Hoffman's
teeth. You don't see the drill enter Hoffman's
mouth, and think: phew! You think: no, no,

no! The question with being burned to death is whether you feel like you do when you touch a hot pan, but worse, and all over, and for ages, or whether, after the moment of engulfment, the pain just sort of becomes like white noise. Drowning, of course, would be different. Being trapped underground, with the water rising; lifting your head to take that last breath as the dark water closes in – that doesn't bear thinking about. So when I say I'm afraid of being in a fire in the Underground, and that this is my worst fear, I don't think actually being burned to death is the most frightening thing. It's the thing that happens before you are burned to death. It's the being trapped. It's the moments of waiting, and of hope. It's the hope. That's the most frightening thing. The hope, and the way it never quite fades.

The train, which definitely smells, but which might not be on fire, might in fact not have any mechanical problems at all, begins to slow down, a sensation I can feel bodily that is also accompanied by a series of squeaking noises, as the brake pads, or whatever, pinch the sides of the wheels, or whatever, and as the train slows down, I know that this deceleration is the prelude to something I have always feared – stopping in the tunnel. When the train stops in the tunnel, I can feel my rational mind, the fine-tuning of its clockwork mechanism, begin to slip, as if it's been over-oiled. The system that takes over, the panic system, is quite different. This system behaves like the stock market at the moment it crashes – people trying to sell what they have, at any price, forcing other people to sell, dumping everything, the mass dumping a cascade of doubt and devaluation. I must not go there. I look around me – and, as I do so, I realize I have, until now, been avoiding any form of contact with other people, in case I can read, from their body language, that they, too, have smelled the burning rubber smell. There is a woman, two seats away from me, and another woman next to her. There's a man in a suit, but no tie, opposite me. He is staring straight ahead – a picture of resolute confidence.

Or absolute terror. I can't tell. Above his head
is the window, and beyond the window, the
wall of the tunnel, lined with cables. Why so
many cables? Each one must be important. If
one were to go wrong – what then? The cables
loom, like the faces I sometimes think I see
when I look out of my ground-floor window
at night. But they are not faces – except in my
head, where they are faces. Above the man's
head is a diagram of the Northern Line, all the
way from Morden to High Barnet and Edgware,
and, to calm myself down, to slow down the
cogs of my mind, I look along the diagram,
at the stations, many of which I know. Things
have happened to me at these stations. Like
Warren Street. That's where I saw the man
talking to himself. And Bank. That's where
I met my friend, who worked in a bank, and
some other bankers, or rather traders, and that's
when I realized that traders were a group unto
themselves, like fighter pilots or marines, with
strange codes of behaviour, like pissing at the
bar, while they were ordering beer, in unison.

Angel – where I lost those documents. The guy had given me two sets of documents, one very important, he said, and one hardly important at all. They were in brown A4 envelopes. My eye goes up and down the list. Bank again – where the bomb went off. I actually heard it; the noise of it spoke to me. Clapham Common. 1987. The last time I ever played football competitively. After that game, I knew it was no use; as a sportsman, I was finished.

In 1987, I wasn't frightened of the Underground. Or hardly frightened. True, I dreaded the moments when the train stopped between stations. I would sit there, scrunched in my seat, trying to stop my mind from slipping into full panic mode, trying to stop the cascade of thoughts and images – the market crash, thoughts giving way to cheaper thoughts, more useless and volatile thoughts. True, sometimes I did not succeed. But the train always started up again – it always cranked back into action. I always reached my destination. I always walked through the concourse and saw the first patch of sky. In 1987, I had not yet reached the point where I could not use the Underground. That came seven years later, in 1994. Why? Trying to answer this question, I draw a blank; I dip my net in the water, and come up with nothing, and I look into the empty, dripping net, and don't want to plunge it in deeper. Freud, I think, said the unconscious was like a big, scary fish in a dark pool: sometimes you see it, and sometimes it breaks the surface, rippling the pool, a sudden, shocking flash of tail and fin, and then it's a dark shape under the surface, and then it's gone. At least I think Freud said that. (My mind is spinning. I must not let it.)

Clapham Common. 1987. I walked out of the station. It was evening. A hot day, the sky overcast and gloomy. A bag slung over my shoulder. I would change in my friend's flat, then walk to the all-weather pitch. All-weather meaning hard. Meaning made out of fine grit. We were to play under floodlights. The opposition were Blackheath rugby team. They had a football team culled from their five rugby

fifteens – the First Fifteen being big beefy guys
who are really good at rugby, pure muscle
and raptor reflexes, the Fifth Fifteen being big
beefy guys who were quite good at rugby. We
changed. We walked to the pitch. It was made
of grit. It was getting dark. The floodlights
were on. The Blackheath guys were wearing
their red rugby shirts. Some of them looked
overweight. Later, somebody told me that
most of them were from the Second and Third
Fifteens. Beefy, competitive guys, seeking more
game-time. I looked at our guys. Intellectuals.
Teachers and lecturers. A slightly overweight
actor. A couple of writers. A guy who worked
for an architecture magazine. Thirty per cent of
us wore glasses on the pitch. But we were good.
We were the Holland team from 1974. Total
football. Great movement off the ball. Passes
you wouldn't believe – passes we didn't believe.
A coin was tossed. We would kick off.

As the striker, I would have the first touch
of the ball. We had this move. I passed to the
guy next to me, and then took off, heading in

the direction of the goalpost to the right of
the goalkeeper. The guy next to me passed it
back to the actor. The actor gave it a touch
or two – and then I jinked across the penalty
area, heading diagonally in the direction of
the other goalpost. The actor looped the ball
in my direction. I turned, and – bang! It almost
never worked. In fact, it never worked, except
in theory.

The whistle went. I touched the ball and took
off, drawing a couple of beefy guys. The actor
had the ball. I jinked. The ball came towards
me. All this happened in three or four seconds.
I could see, exactly, what to do – catch the ball
on the tip of my right foot, cushion it, bring
my right foot, with the ball, backwards, beyond
my left heel, slide the ball sideways – the Cruyff
move – and bang the ball at the goal. This was
it! I was moving backwards and to my right, to
wrong-foot the guy behind me. I could feel his
beefy presence. If you could read my thoughts
at that moment, they would have been: prepare
to witness some real class, Mr Beefy! The ball

was nearing my foot. The move, its absolute precision and perfection, existed Platonically in my mind.

And then the ball touched my foot.

Somehow, I didn't have time to change my body-shape, catch the ball on my toe, drag it back and to the side, turn, and then shoot. I had time – just – to touch the ball with my toe. The beefy guy smashed into me from behind. I don't know exactly what he did. He ran through me. The force of his body lifted me and somehow carried me. He must have been psyching himself up, I thought later. I was flying through the air. I can remember being up there, moving in an arc, unsupported. I also remember the feeling, quite unusual, of falling from a height, and not being at all prepared – no arms in a position to cushion my fall, no flexed feet. Just flying through the air in a random position. And then I was down. The ground had attacked every part of me along one side. As if someone had taken a hammer to my head, my shoulder, my ribcage, my pelvis, and my ankle. The whistle did not go. This was a fair tackle. I started to get up. Seven seconds of the game had elapsed.

We lost, of course. I was hammered, in the same fashion, perhaps fifteen times. Afterwards, I hobbled to a pub and drank four or five pints of beer. When the pub closed, I tried to walk back to my friend's flat. I succeeded. I slept on his sofa. I was not badly injured. Nothing was broken. Nothing was even torn. In the morning, I could not walk very well. I got to Clapham Common Station. This would be my most painful ride on the Underground. The bag with my football gear in it, which I would never wear again, was slung around my shoulder.

Now the train lurches, and begins to move. Then stops. This is the moment that, if I had to bet, I would bet that something really was wrong. But I still don't know for sure. I'm entering a zone of hope. I'm still trying to believe that the burning smell, which has not got worse, and which nobody else seems to have noticed, signifies nothing much. Yet a cold sensation lurches downwards through my body, moving deeper, kicking in my stomach, diving. And then it's gone. Still, the train does not move. The man opposite me does not move either. He retains his resolute, or alternatively horrified, posture. I can see the hairs on his ankles, below the cuffs of his trousers, above the sock-line. One of the women to my left is wearing black trousers, a white blouse, and sandals; the other, an office combo of black skirt, black tights, black shoes. The shoes have a low, clumpy heel. I slide my right hand into my plastic bag, in order to grab my book, in case I need some comfort in the next few moments, and I grab the book, and find that there is not just one book in the bag. There are two. Somehow the idea of taking the second book out, to see what it is, makes me feel nauseous; I think I know what the book is, and it creeps me out. The cogs of my mind are grinding, and beginning to spin.

I often think about the man who was talking to himself on the platform at Warren Street. I know many people talk to themselves – or,

at least, speak without addressing their words
to anybody in particular. There was a man
I saw quite often in the street, I would say he
was about eighty, and every time I saw him,
he was alone, and also speaking out loud. One
day, I slowed down as he approached, to see
if I could hear what he said: there was an odd
moment as I inclined myself towards him, and
I could hear four words. They were: 'hammer
to the head'. This man was shabby; he slouched
and shambled. But the Warren Street man was
quite different. I have never seen a self-talker
who was better presented. I sometimes see
another guy who talks to himself, and wears a
suit, but he also wears an admiral's cap. The
Warren Street guy looked like a politician.
When I got to the platform, the display box
said: 'Edgware 4 mins'. So I knew I had five or
six minutes to wait; a Northern Line minute is a
fungible amount of time, but, in my experience,
it's never less than a minute. A thin crowd had
gathered on the platform. This particular guy
was on the edge of the platform. He wore a

dark suit, very shiny black shoes, and a red tie. He was handsome. He had black hair with a side parting. He might have been a politician. And he was talking to himself.

For the next six minutes, he walked up and down the platform, right on the edge, which made you think he might fall on to the line. He was speechifying. What he was saying was beautifully spoken. He was talking about dates and times. He was making points – semi-coherent points – about how he could remember certain things, but not others. He looked as if he had done what he was doing many times before. Everybody tried not to look at him. Then we got on the train. I didn't see him get on the train.

Once, at Camden Town, I saw that somebody had defecated at the very end of the carriage. There are no toilets on the Northern Line. There are no toilets on the Underground, full stop. I guess it must happen. I was the only person in the carriage. I wondered when the act had taken place. It looked fresh. The smell was awful. I wondered if it had been a man or a woman. I guessed a man.

I remember getting out at Bank Station, in 1990; remember walking up the stairs and along the street, and meeting my friend, the trader, in a bar. He introduced me to the other traders. They wore dark, very expensive suits, the sort of suits Bret Easton Ellis would describe in *American Psycho*: Armani, Cerruti, Valentino. Beautiful shirts and Gucci loafers. We sat at a table and drank lager. As if on cue, four of them walked up to the bar, with empty glasses, held the glasses below the level of the bar, unzipped their flies and started pissing into the glasses. At the same time, one of them ordered four pints of lager. When the fresh pints arrived, they each grabbed a pint of lager in one hand, and replaced it on the bar with a pint of piss. They zipped their flies, turned, and walked back to the table. Then they sat down.

Later, we went to a girly bar in Mayfair. There was a lot of red velvet. The girls were in their underwear. They kept approaching our table and asking us to buy them Champagne. Each time a girl approached, one of the traders, I'll call him Charlie, beckoned her towards him; when she bent down, he said, 'Eat my plop.' After the fourth or fifth girl, the manager came to the table. He said he understood that Mr McKenzie was a good customer, but could he please be more courteous to the girls.

'Eat my plop,' Charlie said.

The manager stood there. He waited a moment. Then he said that, all things considered, it might be a good idea if Mr McKenzie called it a night. He said that Mr McKenzie would be welcome to come back to the establishment any time he liked, but maybe tonight, he'd like to consider going home. The manager said he would have no problem calling Mr McKenzie a taxi.

'Eat my plop.'

The manager went away and returned with two bouncers. He said that, if Mr McKenzie had any difficulty standing up, he had brought some gentlemen to assist him.

'Eat my plop.'

'Very well,' said the manager, 'I have no alternative but to instruct my colleagues to assist you to the door.'

Charlie McKenzie stood up. His eyes were blazing with fury. He walked towards the door. When he got to the door, everybody was watching him. He bowed, a formal sort of bow. He said, 'Eat my plop.' Then he was gone.

A few weeks later, asleep in my bed in north London, I thought I heard something; I was sure I heard something. It had a specific sound that, it seemed at the time, couldn't have been anything else. It was the sound of a political statement, of one side of a political argument. It made me sit up in bed.

Do you know what that sounds like? Believe me, you would if you'd heard it. It had an exact tone, a certain ring to it – not like a car backfiring, or a low-flying jet, or a thunderclap. This was a far deeper, much more percussive sound, a celebrity in the drab crowd of squawks and thuds and wails, of everyday noise pollution.

It came from two miles away. It imprinted itself on my distant ears, carrying with it innuendoes about our history, our foreign policy, our economy.

Boof! That's what it sounded like. Of course, one italicized word can't do it justice – this noise had amazing qualities. It was, actually, the sound of thousands of skyscraper windows, and the windows of bars and restaurants and shops, being broken simultaneously in the vicinity of Bank Underground Station, of a church being de-materialized, of tables and chairs being fragmented into tiny pieces, of the table that Charlie McKenzie's friends were sitting at, and the bar where they ordered their pints of lager, being vaporized, of a crater being forced fifteen feet into the earth. I got out of bed, and thought: right now, at this moment, people will be caught in the teeth of it, this noise, this *message* – they'll be bracing themselves against it, against the bricks, the shards of glass, the paving stones, the office equipment, the stationery, the bits of cars flying through the air. I went downstairs and switched on the radio.

Mad with excitement, the commentators talked it up – they told me about the bomb, the damage, the casualties; as the day went on, and they grew calmer, they sharpened up on their figures, spoke fewer words per minute. They talked about the bomb, carefully avoiding the important subject – the significance of the bomb. It was as if they had received a letter and were telling us about the design of the envelope, the watermark on the writing paper, the colour of the ink the letter was written in. And then, a few days later, the story just stopped, and passed into the category of things that have happened, and are no longer happening – the bomb was upstaged by the shuffling of politicians, the Danish referendum, the Sterling exchange rate, Clinton's haircut; it was over.

Then I went to see the damage. The place was far more smashed up than you would imagine, much more deeply scarred. The bombed area, a great big chunk of London's financial zone, was on the edge of losing its identity. I looked at the pavements, covered in an unfamiliar silt, a post-terrorist topsoil; little lumps of glass, concrete, plaster, chips of wood, cigarette butts and Styrofoam cups. When the wind got up, you saw little eddies of yellow-and-black plastic tape, the sort of tape they use to stretch across the entrances to forbidden places. The litter was printed, not with advertising slogans, but with warnings – flyers with the words 'No hard hat, no entry'; plastic stickers telling you to keep away, to bugger off. But it was a while before I got round to thinking about anything but the surface detail, anything like: what have we done to other people, to make them do this to us? And how can we stop people, if they want to terrorize us?

Well, I thought, we can't. We bombed the Germans. The Germans bombed us. The IRA are bombing us. We bombed Saddam. Then we stopped bombing Saddam. What did the future hold? I had no idea. My mind's eye was always being drawn back towards the thinkable, the prosaic details of the damage.

The trashed area, about the size of the centre of a market town, a few blocks to the east of Bank Station, looked, at best, like a ghetto and, like a ghetto, it was picking up bad habits – when piles of stuff block the walkways of a place, people don't respect them; stacked planks provide a refuge for less legitimate trash. Blind shopfronts, boarded up with corrugated iron and plywood, attract the eye upwards, to the dull, grotty-looking upper halves of the buildings.

The trauma of the explosion did plenty of mechanical damage, but it also attacked the City's modesty: the blast was prying; it was prurient. Stacked on the pavement, you could see the cheap, bulk-bought office furniture of the financial community: the plastic-covered chairs, the low, stained sofas, the sheets of A4 printed with columns of numbers – all the prosaic truth behind the reflecting glass.

Glass. Walking around, I kept wondering

about the constant scraping noise: it was men with dustpans and brushes, working on every floor of every building in a place the size of a small town, sweeping bits of broken glass off the floor. The buildings suddenly looked terrible, now their bluff had been called – now they didn't *reflect*. They looked like poor people's buildings.

'Nobody knows what they're doing,' a man told me. He was wearing a hard hat and goggles. He was a member of a gang clearing 'confidential material' – important documents – from the buildings. His face was covered with a fine layer of plaster dust. 'Up there,' he said, pointing up at one of the wrecked buildings, 'it's bloody awful. Nobody's had any experience of this. Can you imagine being in that place, twenty storeys up, with no windows, when the wind gets up? The floor is just covered with plaster and little bits of glass.'

Yes, I thought, it takes a bit of effort to think of this as part of a political debate. I kept wanting to think about something else. Like the

sale they had in a shoe shop after hundreds of
pairs of shoes were hurled out into the street.
Like the traffic lights that still blinked in the
blocked, useless streets.

Boof! What was that? It was lots of things.
It was a huge bomb in the City. It was placed
in a truck by two men, caught on security
cameras, sneaking away from the truck early
in the morning, their faces deep in the hoods
of their tracksuits. One man died. Important
documents were blown all over town. The
damage cost a billion pounds. It was all over
in a Northern Line minute.

I must not, *must* not, think about the fact
that I'm stuck in a tunnel in a train that is, just
possibly, on fire. I simply refuse to do this. I'd
rather take out one of my books, and plunge
into the world of a maniac financier – or even
the other one, which creeps me out. I have to
face the fact that I keep on reading this book
because it creeps me out. I'd rather turn out my
pockets and examine their contents. I'd rather
think about the time I ran the wrong way up the

escalator at Angel Station in 1978 – traumatic at
the time, but now such a happy, happy thought.
It reminds me of something that happened
to me in 1987, just before my last competitive
game of football. I was moving house – from
south-east London, beyond the reach of the
Underground, to the centre of town, actually in
the shadow of Centre Point. Tottenham Court
Road would be my local station! I hired a van.
It was a Luton van, the biggest thing I'd ever
driven. I had to make two trips. By the evening,
my driving was sketchy. I was tired. The novelty
of moving, of driving a big van, had faded.
I loaded the van up for my second trip. It was
getting dark. I drifted west, and found myself
on a ramp, which led to an elevated dual
carriageway. I took the ramp – and, at last,
I could see where I was going.

The first strange thing I noticed was that a
car was coming at me, very fast, in the wrong
direction, and in my lane. The car honked at
me and swooped away at the last moment. And
then: a coincidence. Another car, again fast,

again in my lane, again honking. These drivers! Driving in London might be the only time I feel any positivity towards the Underground. Next: a batch of cars and vans, all driving fast, all honking – what were the chances of that? They were flashing their lights at me. That made me think. I looked across at the other part of the elevated dual carriageway. A car, going in what looked like the wrong direction – the same direction as me. Unless, of course . . .

1978. The guy, Bradley, gives me two sets of documents. We are in a big warehouse beside a canal in Islington. A ten-minute walk from Angel Station. It's a Friday evening. My task is easy. I must take the documents to a printing firm. A man will be waiting. One document contains the closing prices for thousands of shares on the London Stock Exchange. The printing firm will run off hundreds of copies; a copy will be on every trader's desk in many, many buildings in the City of London by Monday morning. This is the important document. Bradley cannot stress how important this document is. This is a time before email, before fax. You have to take hard copy across town. You entrust the job to a courier. I'm a courier. This is my first important job. Up to now, I've been delivering proofs of birthday and Christmas cards, and get-well cards. Bradley tells me that the other documents are not so important. But I might as well take them anyway. This is his mistake. The other documents are the proofs for Christmas cards. There is a robin on a tree. Bradley marks the important envelope with an 'X'. Otherwise the envelopes are the same. Once again, he tells me of the importance of my task. I shake his hand. I am eighteen.

Walking along the canal path, I understand that to go to a pub and get drunk in this situation would be a mistake. But to have a single drink would, surely, be fine. So I go into a pub. I meet people. Beer splashes on my envelopes. There is a moment when I am torn between being bang on time, or having one last drink. The bonhomie is infectious. The printing plant stays open all night. They need to – they have to – print the City prices. Bonhomie wins.

And then I'm in Angel Station, on the down escalator, watching the tops of people's heads looming up towards me on the other side. I'm moving down, feeling no fear, staring ahead with a glazed expression, calculating my journey time, checking my documents, and I have the document that has not been marked with an 'X', and I'm looking for the document that has been marked with an 'X', and at first I can't find it, and I'm now halfway down the escalator, I look up and there are plenty of people coming down behind me, standing there, staring straight ahead, and I *still* can't seem to find the document that has been marked with an 'X', which might, I now realize, not matter, because now I'm not sure whether that guy Bradley marked the important one or the less important one, the one with the picture of the robin, always an odd thing to put on a Christmas card, robins being desperate predators, always on the edge of starvation, most of them starve, although people don't know this, and I'm near the bottom of the escalator, when I think I know what must have happened; and I know, in my heart, that I've lost the important envelope, know I've taken my eye off the ball, that somewhere I made a wrong turn, and I reason that I must have dropped the important envelope somewhere on this escalator, somewhere near the top, and this is when I turn, and start climbing, looking down at the slatted steps, knocking into the hips and elbows of people, and the climb is harder than I thought, but I grit it out, thinking that, by the time I get to the top, I will find what I'm looking for, but I don't, and the futility of my manoeuvre, trying to find something that could not possibly have fallen upwards, only occurs to me later, after I arrive at the printing firm, after the man designated to meet me has told me off, has sworn at me for being late; after he has ripped open the A4 envelope I give him, and pulled out a document, and looked at it. I can tell from his face it's the robin.

And now the train jolts, and judders, and starts to move, and I am filled with the icy pangs of relief I used to get halfway up the escalator, when I knew I'd see the sky again, when I knew I'd walk across the tiny concourse of whatever station, Angel or Belsize Park or Chalk Farm, and look up, and see a patch of sky, and, even though I can still smell something that is definitely burning rubber, or plastic, I have a sense that everything will be fine, that my fears are all in my head, somewhere in the dark pool, diving deeper; and they have not gone, the fears, but everything seems to be fine, I don't know why I was so frightened of going underground, but maybe those fears were groundless, or perhaps a mechanism I employed to protect me from other, deeper fears, which I have not yet been able to identify, maybe that's why I'm always reading books that creep me out, maybe I am attracted, in some way, to fear, but I've conquered this one; this is what I'm thinking as the jolting and the juddering gives way to a smoother ride, smooth but slow, too slow perhaps, or maybe again it's all in my mind. The woman to my left, the one with the black slacks and the white shirt, or blouse, shifts in her seat and crosses her legs. The man opposite me stares ahead, probably resolutely, I can now see. The train rumbles on. I look out of the window, at the reflections of the people in the train, at the cables on the wall of the tunnel, at the diagram of the stations of the Northern Line. Barnet. Totteridge & Whetstone. I've never been to Totteridge or Whetstone, but I have met Mickie Most, the semi-famous music producer who lives in Totteridge or Whetstone, I can't remember which; I met him during an interview with a pop star, in some studio near Warren Street or Goodge Street; he shook my hand, Mickie Most, and the funny thing is that people seemed more impressed that I'd met Most than the pop star, even though the pop star had topped the charts I think twice, with his very catchy songs. Most's house, sometimes pictured in magazines, is white, and very impressive, with several balconies. And I remember the pop star said something I thought at the time was racist: he said that the Edgware Road was 'like High Street Beirut', meaning it was full of people from the Middle East, and later I wondered why I thought that this was a racist comment; if he'd said it was 'like Fifth Avenue', meaning that it was full of Americans, I would not have thought the comment racist at all. Woodside Park. West Finchley. Mill Hill East. Finchley Central. East Finchley. Highgate. Archway. Tufnell Park. Kentish Town. Hampstead. Belsize Park. Chalk Farm.

'The next station is Chalk Farm.'

I'm staring at the window, at the cables outside the window, and I know that soon, in a few moments, I will see outside light, artificial light certainly, but light coming from outside the train, and this, I have noticed during the three or four journeys since I conquered my fear, always cheers me up, always gives me a boost, particularly if the train has stopped between stations; now, even before this moment happens, I can feel a definite lightening of my spiritual load: the train has momentum, will not stop again before I see the light, and the platform, and the tiles – the very environment that used to frighten me so much, during the period when I was trying to conquer my fear, when I could get on the platform, but no further.

This was a strange time. I would walk out of my flat, turn left, turn left twice, and then right, and in five minutes I'd be at the corner, looking at the front entrance of the station, and at first I'd walk on, with a shudder, and walk up the street, with pasta restaurants on both sides, a curious thing being that on one side of the street, if you asked for your pasta 'al dente', the waiter would nod, and you'd get pasta that was not soft, but on the other side of the street, the waiter would say that he or she was sorry, but the pasta came ready prepared, it was as it was, and he or she had no say in how soft it was. In any case, sometimes I'd walk on, and hail a taxi. But then I started to buy tickets, and get as far as the platform, but no further. And then I got on a train. The doors were about to close, and I leaped on, forcing the issue, and the doors closed behind me, and I felt a terrible suffocating sensation as the train entered the tunnel, and the next minute or so, the next Northern Line minute, seemed to take hours, or days, and then the train pulled into Chalk Farm Station — there was the outside light, there were the tiles — and I wondered why the doors were not opening, thought they might be jammed – *why* were they taking so long to open? – but they slid open, and I darted along the platform towards the lift area. But I didn't wait for the lift. I ran all the way up the stairs. And then the tiny concourse. The patch of sky. At last – I had done it! But would I do it again? At the time, I didn't know.

Yes! We are pulling into the station! All is well! Here it is – the light! I stand up and grab the strap above my head. Now, I can, if I want to, get off the train. But why should I? If I do, I'll be late. To get off here would be a regression. It would set me back. I sit down again. The train stops. There are people on the

43

platform, waiting to get in. The doors open. Two girls, or girly young women, step into the train. One of them says, 'Can you smell something? Like burning?' The other makes a face. There is a moment when they are both making a face. The two girly women sit down. I look at the open doors. Two, three bounds, and I could be gone. The tiny concourse! The sky! The newsagent that sells chocolate bars! I'd be late. But! And I sit there, not bounding across the train, not doing anything, sitting there, clutching my plastic bag, which contains two books, *American Psycho* by Bret Easton Ellis, and *Chappaquiddick Revealed* by Kenneth Kappel, which creeps me out. It's the most frightening Chappaquiddick book, because of its bleak, but, I think, accurate, analysis of human nature. I sit there, clutching my bag, staring at the open doors, and I do nothing; for a long minute I do not act. And I'll remember this long minute, this Northern Line minute, for the rest of my life.

The doors close.

Now that the doors have closed, and there's
no way out, no way out even if I screamed and
banged at the glass, I can feel a pang of regret,
closely followed by a heavier pang of regret,
the pangs moving like an avalanche, crushing
something in me, I have a flash memory of
being in a sauna somewhere, there were other
people in the sauna, and it was hot, but hot
in a way that was not unpleasant, or perhaps
masochistically pleasant, and I wanted to get
out of the sauna, and I stood up, and I tried
the door, but the door was jammed, or seemed
jammed, and I tried again, grabbing at it, it
was definitely jammed, and then the heat of
the sauna seemed to change, from something
pleasant to something beyond unpleasant,
frightening even, and I couldn't breathe, and
I started sweating, strange to say this, because
I was sweating anyway, sweating is the *point*
of a sauna, but sweat was now rolling off me,
my breathing tortured and shallow, and the
heat – the heat! It was different. It was so very
different. And then another guy tried the door,

and he couldn't get it open, and we could see
the door's mechanism, could see how it worked,
or so we thought, but we were stuck, and
frying from the inside, and our brains seemed
to be fried as well. And then the door opened.
The catch had stuck. Shoddy workmanship.
I pushed my way outside; the heat followed me
like a cloud of insects. I didn't feel right all day.
And I worked out how long we thought we were
trapped. It was about a minute.

Desperate not to feel like I did in the sauna,
my mind now beginning to spin, a definite
smell of burning rubber or plastic in my nostrils
(now that those girls have noticed it, it seems
much stronger), I clutch at other thoughts I
might have, any thoughts. Morden. Elephant &
Castle. Borough. The day of Gazza's tears at
Borough. I saw Gazza's tears, that is, in someone's
flat near Borough. Gazza losing control; Gazza
making the lunge that would define him for life.
The lunge – and then the tears, tears of self-pity,
because the referee took out the yellow card,
whipped it out, and this was the semi-final of

the World Cup, and now that Gazza was booked,
whatever else happened, he would not play in
the final, would certainly be remembered, but
as a bit-part player – would not be, as the cultural
critic Paul Morley memorably said, 'in the magic
eleven', the players who would play in the
final, who would become the magic eleven if
they won the World Cup, like the magic eleven
from 1966, I can remember them, my mind
is spinning, let's see, Banks, Cohen, someone,
Stiles, Charlton, someone, yes, Moore of course,
Ball, Hunt, Hurst, someone, Peters; I'm sitting
here, waiting for the train to move, smelling the
smell, and I can't remember the magic eleven!
I've always been able to remember the magic
eleven! And now I can only remember nine.
This is what I'm thinking as the train moves
out, Wilson, I'm thinking, Ray Wilson, wasn't
he the undertaker, but that still only makes ten,
I'm thinking.

Come on; come *on*, I'm thinking, as the
avalanche deepens, as the fear sends new shoots
through my brain, growing fast, like bamboo,

everything is fine, *it is just my imagination*. Get a grip. Idiot! I look at the two women, the girly women, opposite me; their heads are close together. Their body language does not bode well. I shift in my seat, as the platform moves past. The women sitting opposite me, directly in my line of vision, are attractive, but they couldn't be models, because they are shaped like normal women; I remember once sitting on a train at I think Tottenham Court Road, and two models got on, you often see models at Tottenham Court Road; these women had that look of flamingoes, too tall and all sharp angles, and they were clutching their portfolios, doing what they do all day, traipsing around London, showing people pictures of themselves, and I realized that these models were less attractive than all the other women in the carriage, and then I realized that, in fact, models are not actually attractive – they just look attractive in photographs. Somebody once told me that this was the thing to bear in mind if you wanted to date models – that they are not, in the end,

48

very attractive. He said the upside was that, when you split up, which would be very soon, you got to keep photographs of the person, which actually did look attractive, and which would fool most people who looked at them. Even though, he said, they didn't fool him, because he was an expert.

Is it my imagination, or is the train moving very slowly indeed? Is it my imagination, or is the smell of burning getting stronger? Is it my imagination, or is this train on fire? Is it my imagination, or am I in a fire, in a tunnel, on the Northern Line, between Chalk Farm and Camden stations?

Why did I not get off at Chalk Farm? Not getting off at Chalk Farm was stupid, like Gazza's lunge; and, yes, it was impulsive, even though it was an impulse *not* to do something. There he is, as the clock winds down, in the semi-final of the World Cup, the match between England and Germany a stalemate, and the German player Berthold has the ball, going nowhere in particular, and Gazza, psyched up, launches himself at Berthold, sliding along, crunching through him, and the whistle goes, and, for a minute, Gazza loses it, his face and body language a pantomime of regret, his brain an avalanche of bad, roiling thoughts, a market crash of volatility, dumping everything he can; his pride, his self-respect, his ability to function normally, and the head bows, the face scrunches up. And then the tears. And people said, afterwards, how weird and unsettling it was that these tears, this loss of control, made Gazza into a national treasure, which said a lot, didn't it, about the nation that came to treasure him.

The train is slow, painfully slow; it's moving, but only just, and I wonder what's above me, but I don't want to think about it, don't want to think about the street, or the park, or the nearby zoo, the elephants and lions, but I can't help thinking about the elephants and lions; if I'd chosen to walk, instead of taking the Underground, right now I'd be walking in a park, looking at elephants and lions, and

I'd be able to buy a coffee in the park, and I could blow out my film, it's only work, it's not life itself, and I could sit down on a bench, in the mild sunshine, and read my book about Chappaquiddick.

Of course, it's in my bag, and I could take it out now, and pretend I'm sitting on a bench in the park, with a view of elephants, pretend everything is fine, that the smell of burning is not getting stronger, that the people around me are not shuffling and scrunching themselves up in their seats, which they are, their body language looks ominous now; I could pretend to myself that this is one of those moments like when you're alone in a house, at night, and the plumbing makes noises, like it sometimes does, sounding like someone clumping through the house, someone with an odd, broken, rattling gait, and you say to yourself, that's funny, if I didn't know that this noise was coming from the plumbing, I'd be really scared right now, and then a minute goes by and you are in a new world – you *are* really scared, even though you know it's the plumbing, too scared, say, to see any humour in the situation, and you can't bear to look out of the window, and you draw the curtains, and check the doors are locked, even though you know, in your heart, that everything is really fine.

I could pretend to myself that this is one of those moments.

So I hunker down in my seat, and I don't look up, not at all, and I take my book out of my bag, and I imagine I'm sitting on a park bench, lost in my book, which is a small, battered paperback, the sort with sensational pictures on the front, the edges of the pages dyed yellow. It's the story of a man who made a terrible mistake. The mistake defined his life. The mistake defined our lives. The man was Ted Kennedy – younger brother of JFK and RFK. The mistake was that he went out with a young woman in a car, and had a few drinks. The young woman was not his wife. His wife was pregnant. He had an accident in the car. He did not report the accident. The young woman died. Which meant that he had no chance of becoming president. And this is why our lives might be different.

Oh, the regrets he must have had! This book is compulsive – it's part of a genre I think of as regret porn. And what could be better than to spend a happy morning reading regret porn, sitting on a park bench, with dangerous wild animals in cages just yards away. Here are the facts. It's a gorgeous morning. The leaves are coming out. The sun is bright. But it's not too hot. There are clouds in the sky. But it won't rain. I'm sitting on a lacquered bench, in a perfect spot – shaded by a tree. Probably a maple, but I can't say for sure. I'm next to a path, which I sometimes jog along. I'm very happy, for some reason, to have taken the morning off. Behind me, as I say, are elephants, lions, leopards and tigers. Sometimes I can hear the big cats snarling and making guttural noises. I don't even flinch. To the south – a road. But I can only hear a faint whine from the traffic. Above me, planes move in their holding pattern as they prepare to land at Heathrow. Below me, trains clatter along in tunnels, so far below I'm not even aware of them. In my hands – a book about a man who made a terrible decision, and killed someone, and got away with it.

I decide to forget about my environment, wonderful though it is, and concentrate on the book. But I can't. Something seems to be distracting me. I place the book on my lap, its spine cracked, the yellow edges of the pages just visible. I've read it lots of times before, anyway. Something happened one night in the summer of 1969. Senator Edward Kennedy went to a regatta on Martha's Vineyard, an island off the coast of Massachusetts. Then he went to a party in a house on the smaller Chappaquiddick Island, which can be reached from Martha's Vineyard by a ferry. At the party, he met Mary Jo Kopechne, an attractive blonde woman who had worked for his brother Robert. Ted drove her away from the party in a car. And here, the facts become fuzzy. He had been drinking. There was some kind of accident. He did not report the accident. The next morning, the car was found in the sea. It was upside down. Mary Jo's body was in the car. She had drowned. But she'd lived a long time, trapped in the upside-down car, breathing from a pocket of air in the car's footwell.

I shudder. I pick up the book again, and flip through its pages. Kennedy's claim was that he drove off the edge of a causeway, into the sea, and somehow got out of the sinking car, and 'dove repeatedly' to save Mary Jo – but, when he couldn't do this, instead of reporting the accident, he sat on the bank for a while, walked across the island, swam to Martha's Vineyard, went to sleep in his hotel room, woke up, had breakfast, and then remembered he'd driven a car off the edge of a causeway with a woman inside. That's his story. That's the best he can do. Under any form of close examination, his story falls apart. Almost nothing makes sense.

Just looking at these pages, with the pictures of the funeral, documents from the legal battle about whether or not Mary Jo's body should have undergone an autopsy, diagrams of blood-spatter, photographs of the recovered car, gives me a sense of moment, of something big happening, which it's supposed to do – and Kappel has interpreted the facts in a way that makes Kennedy's behaviour very sinister indeed. Judging from the evidence, as Kappel says, only one thing can have happened – drunk, Kennedy crashed his car; Mary Jo was knocked unconscious. She had a wound to the head. She was bleeding. She would need a doctor. The incident would reach the media – so no presidency. But what if . . .

Sitting on this bench, something jolts me out of my reverie – but it's something I can't bear to think about. I bring my book closer to my face. Where was I? What if. What if Kennedy and his associates pushed the car, and the girl, into the sea? What if he said he tried to save her? What if he waited until there was no alcohol in his blood? What if he said he'd become dazed and confused? What if he waited until the next morning to report the accident? What

if he arranged for the car to be towed away
and crushed? What if he used his contacts to
make sure there was no autopsy? A huge task
lay ahead of him. And he did everything – he
ticked all the boxes. And he stayed out of jail.
But nobody really believed him. He could never
successfully run for president. It was no use.
No use! That's what he must have thought, over
and over again. It was no use! It didn't work!
In the end, he had to face reality. How many
times, I'm wondering now, has he woken up,
having dreamed that he didn't go to the party,
or that he did go to the party but didn't have
anything to drink, or that he did go to the party,
did drink, but decided not to drive, or that he
did drink, did drive, and reported the accident
straight away, Mary Jo being rushed to hospital,
and surviving, his presidential hopes in tatters.
But it didn't make any difference anyway – that
was the point.

I look at the pictures in the centre of the
book, at the drawing of Mary Jo in her final
position, gasping for her last few breaths, upside

down in the footwell of the car, as the car sinks, as the water level rises, and I close the book, and I bend my head, and I'm on a train, on the Northern Line, in a tunnel, between Chalk Farm and Camden Town, knowing that something is wrong, the smell more acrid now, the train moving at an odd, slow, rattling pace, and I open the book, and look at the drawing again, of Mary Jo, and think of the description of how she was when they found her, she'd stiffened up, and I peek to the sides of my book, in this dim tunnel, and people are moving oddly now, still unwilling to reveal their panic to each other, but they know they are trapped, or possibly trapped, I can feel that something here has changed, although still going through a charade of decorum, still not talking to each other, even the two girlish women, who are looking away from each other, but you can tell, you can tell from the hands, the hands and the feet, that something is deeply wrong.

Me! This is happening to me! A person who always shied away from danger. A person

who hated cliff paths, glass lifts, high towers.
Who never went in caves – and I knew people
who went into caves, they said it was safer than
driving, and I'm sure they were right – but
driving was also something that frightened
me. But I drove. And I flew. And then, about
two years ago, I developed a specific phobia,
a phobia of the Underground, because I *hated*
being in tunnels, *hated* getting stuck in tunnels,
felt very strongly about it, but I didn't listen,
did I? I listened to other things. Like, when
Saddam invaded Kuwait, and we invaded Iraq,
us and the Americans, and I was working for
a newspaper, and we were told to report to the
editor for our war assignments, and I said, right
then, that I wasn't going, that nobody could
make me, that I'd resign first, I'd rather chuck
my job than go somewhere where I was in
harm's way, and the next day, I got out of the
Underground at Old Street, near the newspaper;
I wasn't particularly afraid of the Underground
then, this was 1991, and I went to see the editor
in his office. There were two people ahead of

me. The first one came out. He'd been sent to the Gulf. The second guy came out. Gulf again. Then it was my turn. I was ready to chuck it all in. I really was. He told me he wanted me to provide an American point of view. I asked him where he wanted to send me, because I'd been thinking about this, and, in fact . . .

'America,' he said.

I looked at him. I nodded. It was, I said, something I'd love to do. And, later, as I put my ticket into the automatic machine at Old Street, as I stood on the platform, and as I sat down on the train, I was ecstatic – to be going somewhere where there were hotels, sports bars, domestic and imported beers, room service, TV, movies and bookshops (in one of which I would buy Kenneth Kappel's book *Chappaquiddick Revealed*, which made me think that, if Ted Kennedy had not had those drinks, or had had those drinks and had not driven, he might have run for president in '88, and might have won, and, as he said later, if it had been his decision, he would not have invaded Iraq in '91), and let's not forget decent restaurants. Rather than a hot, dry, inhospitable place full of bombs, and guns, and tanks, and armoured vehicles, and explosions, and fires, and thick, black, oily smoke.

The train eases to a stop. It hasn't been moving fast. There is smoke in the tunnel, and it's permeating the train. This is my guess. But why? What's on fire? Is this the same fire I could smell? I look up. I am now prepared to meet another person's eye. I am not yet ready to do anything further, such as kick at the glass. But why? Don't know. Is this the same smoke? Is this . . . the man across from me coughs. I look at him. He looks away. I can't *believe* this. I am *angry*. I am *furious*. Who would have thought? Three million people take the Northern Line every day, I think, three million people, and how many die in fires every year? Answer: none. That's three million times a hundred times three and a half, which is, let me see, how many journeys is that? – a billion, that's how much, give or take, a billion journeys a year and no fires, a billion journeys a year and no deaths, that's like, what, twenty lotteries, by God I'm going to play the lottery if I get out of here – a billion! I breathe, and, for the first time, feel the acrid sensation in my throat as well as my nose.

Why didn't I get off at Chalk Farm? Why not? Two, three bounds and I would have been out – two or three bounds, then a jog up the spiral staircase – or I could have waited for the lift! The doors open. I get in. The doors close. I ride to the surface in comfort. And then the tiny concourse. The patch of sky. The chocolate bar. The walk along Regent's Park Road. The bench in the park. The zoo. The coffee in the cardboard cup. Forget the film. I'll see the film another day. Why did I not do that? I was already standing up, knew in my bones that something was wrong – and I sat down again! Why?

My fury grows. I am angry because I have no alternative. Or, rather, because I will not have any truck with the alternative. I don't want to be full of fear, and dread, and desperate hope.

Spare me the hope! I am so angry with myself. Why did I come down here at all? Something is desperately wrong when people, for whatever reason, decide to travel in underground tunnels when there are perfectly good alternatives. Why would they want to do this? The smoke is thicker now. People are coughing. I had no idea – but it's so obvious! Why did I not think of this before? It makes no sense – absolutely no sense; I should tell people. It's only just occurred to me. But it's a major discovery. I feel like Galileo. Underground tunnels – this is, is . . .

And now I'm putting my face in my hands, breaking out of formation, the first in the carriage to adopt a position of open despair. We are in the penultimate carriage. The carriage is not even half full. We are towards the back of the train. These are the facts. The train is not moving. This is a fact. We are 150 feet below Chalk Farm Road, right on the border between Chalk Farm and Camden, by Camden Market, that place I don't much like but would give anything to be in right now, wandering around, fingering cheap trinkets, whatever. This is a fact. I think we might not get out of here. Another fact. All these facts. I am armed with facts. I was, it turned out, right not to want to come down here. At least there's that! I was right – and everybody else was wrong. But who is down here, in the smoky tunnel? Me, who was right. Another fact: the train is not moving.

My options this morning: stay in bed. Get up early, walk through the park, and see the film. Get up early, have breakfast, sit in garden. Get up early, have breakfast in café, hail taxi, go to see film. Forget film, walk to park, sit on bench, read book. Go on long walk. Stay at home and watch daytime TV. Do my taxes. Clear out cupboards. Pay bills. See my bank manager. Go into a tunnel where there's a fire. That's, let's see, a 92 per cent chance of not being in a fire in a tunnel. The train is still not moving. I have never been stuck in a tunnel this long. I have never smelled so much smoke in an Underground train. So there must, there *must*, be a fire in the tunnel. There *must*.

Now there's a noise. The door opens. The noise is the noise of coughing. A man comes through the door. He is the person who is coughing. Smoke comes through the door. The door closes. The man moves through the carriage. He moves through our carriage, the penultimate carriage. The man has made smoke come into our carriage. The smoke is on the other side of the door. The smoke is in the next carriage. It smells of burning rubber, or burning plastic. It smells of oil and metal. Somewhere beyond the next carriage, things are being singed and charred. The door opens again. Another man comes through the door. This man is coughing too. He closes the door behind him. He lets more smoke in. He runs through our carriage. He runs into the next carriage.

The timetable. It's all wrong. Everything happens very, very slowly. But it's all over very quickly. People are pushing through the door. Two come through. Four come through. Five come through. Smoke comes through. There is

65

coughing. I am coughing. The smoke is thicker on the other side. Some people are still sitting down. I try to stand up, but somebody knocks me down. A beefy man, who might almost be the man who knocked me down the last time I played football seriously; his face has thickened up, he's coughing, he's wearing a Gore-Tex jacket, and I stand up again, clutching my bag, and more people are coming through, and another man knocks me back, there is a river of men coming through, some women but mostly men, I can see their hands and their necks, flesh spilling over seams, bad shoes, cheap shirts, hair gone wrong, teeth, mouths open, choking. Everybody wanting to move.

More smoke is coming.

People are not quite panicking. They are on the edge of panic. But they are not quite panicking. I'm quite impressed. This is quite orderly. This is good. Orderly.

I'm in a train, in a tunnel, and there's a fire, and I'm trapped, and smoke is coming into the carriage, and it's not stopping, and

people are coming into the carriage, and they
are not stopping, and I am not thinking about
my chances of getting out alive, cannot at all
go there in my mind, not at all, I keep trying
to stand up, so I can go into the end carriage,
so I can go where the others want to go, the
promised land where there is less smoke,
but I can't, there's a steady stream of people,
of knees, elbows, chins, and the man across
from me, the resolute man, says, 'Sit down,
everybody!' and I stay seated, while the promised
land fills up, and now people from the front,
smokier, end of the train are beginning to fill up
our carriage too; we have become the promised
land, fancy that, now everyone wants to be
in our carriage, me and the resolute man, the
woman in the white shirt, the woman with the
clumpy shoes, and the two girly women, who,
when I can see them, which I can intermittently,
look shocked, faces in a rictus; we may not be
in the prime location, but our price seems to be
rising, here we are, filling up, one man in front
of me has a handkerchief in his hand, another

with a grey suit and tie, the new neighbours; and I *will not* let my mind drift towards the future, I am looking at the people, looking for orderliness, for who is orderly and who is not: here is a handsome man in a suit, with a side parting in his hair; he is orderly, here is a man in a fleece; he is orderly too, they are taking their places, the opened door of course allowing more smoke into the carriage, which makes things much worse, but seems less of an affront – and, now that the carriage is filled with people, it's quite extraordinary how little space there is around me, and I think: but I have a seat, I have a seat, and there is air, and I can breathe it.

There is a voice coming from the next carriage – from the promised land. It's a woman speaking into a megaphone. I can't hear what she is saying. She keeps saying the same thing. Then I can hear what she is saying. We will evacuate the train and move down the tunnel in the direction of Chalk Farm.

Then she says: 'Stay where you are.'

Then she says: 'The driver will attempt to take the train into Camden Town Station.'

I do not feel saved. I feel trapped. I feel more trapped now than I did before; now I have allowed a chink of sunlight to enter my mind. A moment ago, I was thinking of smoke, and orderliness; now I'm thinking that the train might start to move; any minute the train might start to move. But the train does not move. The train stays still. Which does not make me feel saved. Which makes me feel trapped.

The train rattles. Then the train judders. Then nothing.

Perhaps there is less smoke than there was. Or perhaps not.

I am looking up, at trousers, at fabric.

The people in my carriage are nowhere to be seen. Other people are in the way.

The train judders. Then it moves. Then it stops.

Then it moves.

This is a different style of movement. We've had slow movement. But this is very slow movement. This is the movement of a big old galleon. We are making stately progress. But we are not stopping.

And now, we stop. We're in the station. I couldn't see it, that's all. But we must be in the station. I want to believe it. The area above my head is lighter. People are shifting. Nothing happens for a while. Then the doors open. We are in a station, and the doors are open. I begin to worry about being crushed by people. I had not thought of that! I'd been concentrating on the smoke.

The first people start to get out. The people in my carriage start to thin out. They are orderly. Now I can see the girly women. We do not look at each other. The woman with the white blouse stands up. The woman with the clumpy shoes stands up.

I stand up. I am stiff. I feel wrecked. I feel angry. Why am I angry? I am saved.

Now it's my turn to walk through the doors. The doors will be open until everybody is off. I can tell that. Not like normal, when they close after a short period of time, whether you are ready or not. This is a concession. They are making a concession for us.

On the platform, I can hear a man saying to another man, 'It was the brakes. It was the brakes. The brakes.' I walk along the platform. I look up at the digital display. It says: 'Morden via Charing Cross 1 min'. A sign says 'Way Out'.

And I step on to the escalator, and I wonder what I will do next, and I can't think of what I want to do. I have no idea what I want to do. It's a long escalator. I make a vow never to travel on the Underground again, a vow I will break and reinstate several times. Travelling through tunnels in London, it turns out, is a pretty good way to get around. If you live in London, those tunnels will become part of your life.

On the escalator, I'm thinking: I was right! That was smoke.

And: That was terrible.

And: That was not too bad.

And: I came through that pretty well.

And: That resolute man! He was so cool!

And: I was right! It was smoke!

And: I am saved!

And: Yes!

And: This escalator!

And: How long is this taking?

It takes a minute, a Northern Line minute,
to get to the top of the escalator. At the ticket
machine, they still expect me to have my ticket.
Nobody up here seems to know what has
happened to me. My ticket is deep in the pocket
of my jeans. I realize I probably could not get
a refund. I walk out of the station, and into the
street. Then I walk a few blocks north, retracing
my underground route.

I walk past the market I wished I was in.
I don't wish I was in it now. I walk across the
road, and stand above the point where I think
we were stuck. I look down at the pavement.

A few hundred yards up the road is Chalk
Farm Station, where I should have got off –
where, in my new life, I would get off. I buy

a bar of chocolate at the station newsagent.
I cross the road, and then the bridge. I walk
along Regent's Park Road, across Primrose
Hill, and into Regent's Park.

The elephants are not there. But I can see
some lemurs. I sit down on a bench. I think of
the moment I got on the train, the moment the
doors closed, the moment I did not get off at
Chalk Farm. When the people came rushing in.

I take my book out. I place it in my lap. The
cracked spine; the yellow edges of the pages.
I think of the escalator. I think of the concourse.

I look at the sky, and feel the need to cry.

PENGUIN LINES

Choose Your Journey

If you're looking for...

Romantic Encounters

Heads and Straights
by Lucy Wadham
(the Circle line)

Waterloo–City, City–Waterloo
by Leanne Shapton
(the Waterloo & City line)

Tales of Growing Up and Moving On

Heads and Straights
by Lucy Wadham
(the Circle line)

A Good Parcel of English Soil
by Richard Mabey
(the Metropolitan line)

Mind the Child
by Camila Batmanghelidjh and
Kids Company
(the Victoria line)

The 32 Stops
by Danny Dorling
(the Central line)

A History of Capitalism
According to the Jubilee Line
by John O'Farrell
(the Jubilee line)

A Northern Line Minute
by William Leith
(the Northern line)

Mind the Child
by Camila Batmanghelidjh and
Kids Company
(the Victoria line)

Heads and Straights
by Lucy Wadham
(the Circle line)

**Laughter and
Tears**

**Breaking
Boundaries**

Drift
by Philippe Parreno
(the Hammersmith & City line)

Buttoned-Up
by Fantastic Man
(the East London line)

Waterloo–City, City–Waterloo
by Leanne Shapton
(the Waterloo & City line)

Earthbound
by Paul Morley
(the Bakerloo line)

Mind the Child
by Camila Batmanghelidjh
and Kids Company
(the Victoria line)

The Blue Riband
by Peter York
(the Piccadilly line)

**A Bit of
Politics**

The 32 Stops
by Danny Dorling
(the Central line)

*A History of Capitalism
According to the Jubilee Line*
by John O'Farrell
(the Jubilee line)

**Musical
Direction**

Heads and Straights
by Lucy Wadham
(the Circle line)

Earthbound
by Paul Morley
(the Bakerloo line)